How to Eat Good

In A **Bad** Economy

Buddy Brown

authorHOUSE®

AuthorHouse™
1663 Liberty Drive, Suite 200
Bloomington, IN 47403
www.authorhouse.com
Phone: 1-800-839-8640

Published by AuthorHouse 6/12/2013

ISBN: 978-1-4389-3889-9 (sc)
ISBN: 978-1-4817-6617-3 (e)

Printed in the United States of America
Bloomington, Indiana

This book is printed on acid-free paper.

Contents

Introduction

Dear Fellow Food Lovers,

Welcome to How to Eat Good in a Bad Economy. I, like most of you, like to eat good. I also love to cook. Unfortunately, like millions of us, eating well in this economy is not always easy. After filling our gas tanks, paying our mortgage, electric, and water bills, there isn't much money left over for food.

That's why I put this recipe collection together. God wanted us to eat good and He doesn't much care about the economy. However, We need to. The recipes include a lot of chicken and less expensive cuts of meat and pork. Adding the other ingredients and techniques that I will show you, will add big flavor to a small food budget.

Feeding your family healthy, nutritious and delicious food is fun and easy. It starts in the sale flyers from your local grocery stores. I like to eat fresh. This means I end up in the market just about every day. I get the freshest ingredients I can also find out if they have re-packaged yesterdays food. Be careful. If the top sirloin is gray, buy the fish. If the fish smells like anything but the sea, make your own pasta. One last point. I prefer fresh vegetables, but canned are perfectly fine for most of these recipes, but cooking times will vary.

Seasoning, marinating, smoking and saucing adds big flavors to food. (If you are smoking outside, it makes your neighborhood smell good, too.) This book contains recipes and instructions to give food big and bold flavors on a small budget. There are some very popular sauces on the market that are more expensive and less healthy than if you make them yourself, and contain ingredients than I can't pronounce. Asian duck sauce is a perfect example. There are 5 ingredients in my recipe, 13 in the commercial ones, and the extra 8 ingredients do nothing for the flavor or texture.

The recipes in this book are my ideas on how to make food taste great. Some of them are time consuming, but I think you will find that the dishes are worth the effort. Try mine, and then experiment. A recipe is a guideline, not a rule. You may not like the ingredients I've put in a recipe. If that's the case, use something else, or leave it out completely. Whatever you decide, eat well, have fun, and share food with friends and family.

God Bless You and Your Family,

Buddy Brown

P.S. Thank you for buying the book.

Notes on Chile Peppers

Chile peppers add tremendous amounts of flavor, as well as heat to food. Most chiles have a fruity and sweet side as well. Depending on how you prepare them will determine how much heat they will give to a dish. Most of the heat comes from the ribs and the seeds, so if you want a lot of heat, use the whole pepper, except the stem.

Chile peppers are an inexpensive way to bring out big flavors. When used in a marinade, the heat spreads evenly throughout the food, creating a nice kick, but not a bite that will burn someone. Roasting chilies before putting them to use, brings a nice fruity heat to a dish.

Most of the time I only use 3 types of chiles, but you can use whatever you have. Dried chiles can be substituted for fresh, and the same goes for fresh. Chile peppers vary drastically in the amount of heat, so when substituting, it's a good idea to start with a milder pepper and increase the heat to taste.

The following is a partial list of chile peppers listed in order of mildest to hottest.

	Heat Rating
Bell	1
Cuban Elle	1
Mini Sweet	1
Mild Cherry	1
Anaheim	2
Poblano	3
Jalapeno	5
Serrano	6
Finger Hut	7
Scotch Bonnett/Habanero	10

WARNINGS:

When working with chiles, I recommend using gloves. Chiles will hurt you. Never Touch your eyes or any open cuts. Wash your knives and cutting surfaces with hot water before moving to other preparations.

When preparing poultry, always clean your cutting boards and utensils before using them for anything else. Cook until the internal temperature is 175 degrees.

Smoking

Cooking food on an open fire brings out and adds tremendous amounts of flavor and juiciness. Smoking food on an open fire with wood chips smoldering underneath for hours is the oldest, and in my opinion, the best way to cook food. Smoking gives to food an earthy flavor that I believe used to already be in foods until over farming and over grazing. You can smoke food using a gas grill, charcoal grill, a stovetop smoker, or you can build a hearth. (Instructions for the latter are available in most hardware stores and on the Internet.) You can smoke anything, beef, pork, poultry, vegetables, and so on. The question isn't can I smoke it; it is why shouldn't I smoke it.

Indirect heat is just as important as the smoke in the cooking process. This means you want the heat to permeate the smoke from the smoking wood chips in and around the food to be smoked, but not cook the food quickly. Smoking can take up to 8 hours depending on what you're smoking.

Smoking with a gas grill.

This is the easier way to get the job done. One hour before smoking, soak your wood chips in water. When ready to smoke, remove one of the grates and preheat that side of your grill to the right temperature. When ready to smoke, preheat your grill. The ideal temperature is between 200-225 degrees. While the grill is heating, make a few foil pouches with the soaked wood chips by placing the foil on a flat surface. Place a handful of wood chips in the center of the foil. Fold the foil into a ball about the size of a tennis ball. Using a fork, poke a few holes in the foil to allow the smoke to escape. Place a couple of the pouches directly on the burners on the heated side of your grill. Place a disposable foil pan with a couple on inches of water in it under the grate on the cool side of the grill. Place the food to be smoked on the grate over the foil pan. Close the lid and let the smoking begin. You will need to remove the foil pouches when they start to burn, and replace them with new ones every 20-30 minutes, depending on what is being smoked.

Smoking with a Charcoal Grill

This method takes longer, but I believe that food tastes better when smoked this way. Note: Never use charcoal, lighter fluid, or those solid charcoal starters. That is what your food will taste like. Instead, use hardwood lump charcoal and a chimney starter.
Hardwood charcoal is chinks of wood that have been slightly charred, imparting a flavor on food that is absolutely to die for. A chimney starter is a cylinder of aluminum with 2 compartments and wholes in the bottom. Both are available at the hardware store.

To light the wood chunks, turn the chimney starter upside down and fill the compartment with rolled up paper bags, leaving enough space for air to circulate. You can use newspaper to light the lump charcoal, but I don't know if the ink adds unappealing flavor. Turn the chimney starter over, and fill this compartment with the wood chunks. Place the starter in a safe place. Using a candle lighter or a long match, place the lighter through the holes and light the paper evenly. Leave the starter alone until the coals have a gray surface.

When the coals are gray, on one side of the grill, carefully pour the hot coals in as small a pile as possible. Put the grate back in the grill, and place the food to be smoked on the other side of the grill and close the lid. Every 2 beers, or 20-25 minutes, lift the lid and check the heat. If the food is smoking too fast, block off more air into the grill. The more airflow, the more heat. Remember, you want the temperature between 200 and 225 degrees.

Smoking with a Stovetop Smoker

Smoking this way is the only safe way to smoke indoors. If you have a stovetop smoker, you can achieve a reasonable amount of flavor in less than half the time. Of the three, gas smoking, hardwood smoking, and stovetop, I think you will find that hardwood smoking is the best, flavor wise and juiciness.

Barbecue

The term barbecue used to mean cooking on a flame, with high heat using charcoal or wood. True barbecuing is a process of using a spice rub, smoking, and basting with a sauce in the last stages of cooking, on an open flame. The recipes in this book take you step by step to true barbecuing.

The rule of thumb is if it can be broiled in an oven or broiler, it can be barbecued Barbecuing will give the food a much deeper level of flavor and juiciness that broiling will never match. This means that we may use less expensive cuts of meat, pork, and poultry, and be rewarded with big and bold flavors.

Note: If you are not a fan of smoked flavor, or you don't have a couple of hours, fast cooking on a flame built with hardwood charcoal will give you just a hint of smokiness, but all the juiciness.

Safety Tips

1. Place the grill away from the house, bushes and dry grass. My grill is on my deck as far from the house as possible. I use the chimney starter on a marble slab which rests on a concrete slab.
2. Make sure the grill will not fall over.
3. Stay with the chimney starter and grill as soon as you fire it up. Bring your beer and food with you. Do not leave unattended, and be careful of pets and drunk guests.

Do's and Don'ts

1. Never use any grill indoors, or inside boats, campers, tents, garages, or a completely closed space. The wood or gas will use up the oxygen leaving deadly carbon monoxide.
2. Never use lighter fluids, solid starters, butane torches, gasoline, kerosene, or alcohol. The safest and tastiest way to ignite wood is the chimney starter. When using a gas grill or stovetop smoker, always follow the manufacturers instructions and safety tips.
3. Never add volatile liquids such as alcohol to the fire. Flare-ups can cause major burns and or explosions.
4. When adding more hardwood or soaked woodchips, use tongs to remove the used ones and add the new.
5. Keep a spray bottle full of water nearby to control flare-ups and slow the coals down if they get to hot.
6. To lower the temperature, open the lid and spread the wood chunks apart. To raise the heat, close the lid or push the chunks together.
7. Despite popular belief, Never, Never, Never pierce the food. All this does in open the flesh and spew out all the juices leaving you and old shoe. To check the temperature

of the fire, hold your hand over the coals at cooking height. If you can only hold you hand there for 2-3 seconds, your fire is high, above 375 degrees. 4-5 seconds is medium, about 300 degrees. 6-7 seconds is low, between 200-250 degrees. Ideal for slow roasting or smoking.

8. When using the chimney starter, if you're looking to smoke, when the coals are red hot halfway up the cylinder, they are at about 200 degrees. If you're looking for medium heat, when the flames are visible at the top of the cylinder, they're ready. If you need high heat, let the top coals form a gray ash.
    Dump the coals into the grill and close the lid. Let the coals burn for at least 15 minutes so they will heat up evenly.

9. Buy steaks at a minimum of 1 inch thick. Anything less, will dry out even when cooking to medium rare.

10. When making hamburgers, make them at least 1 inch thick because they will dry out as well.

11. Live to eat. Don't eat to live. The Italian culture marries friends, family, the earth and food in such a beautiful way. Food should be shared with friends and family, with a deep appreciation for God, the earth, and the sea. Americans have only lost that ideal because we let it. Everything gets in the way of sharing meals with our friends, neighbors and family. Sunday dinner in most American homes is based on what happens each and every day in Italy. I sincerely hope that since some of these recipes take a while, that we as Americans bring back some of that Italian ideal. At least once a week would be cool.

Seasoning Blends and Spice Rubs

Every cook has their own spice mixture for seasoning foods and spice rubs for barbecue. So do I. For everything but barbecue, I almost exclusively use Chef Emeril Lagasse's original Creole Seasoning. I have been using it for 11 years now, and I find it is the perfect seasoning for anything Chef Lagasse's seasoning blends are available commercially, as are many other good ones, but I prefer to mix my own. This way I know how fresh the ingredients are. If I am making an ethnic dish, I use a mixture indigenous to that region, such as a Texas rub for Texas Barbecue. The following is my idea of the best the world has to offer.

Chef Lagasses's original Creole seasoning

Caribbean Jerk Rub

Southwestern Rub

Texas Rub

Kansas City Rub

Italian Seasoning

Chef Emeril Lagasse's Original Creole Seasoning

2 1/2 tbls sweet paprika
2 tbls kosher salt
2 tbls garlic powder
1 tbls freshly ground black pepper
1 tbls onion powder
1 tbls cayenne pepper
1 tbls dried thyme
1 tbls dried oregano

Place all the ingredients in an airtight container. Put the lid on and shake well until well mixed. Will keep in an airtight container for up to 6 months.

Caribbean Jerk Rub
2 tbls ground coriander
2 tbls granulated ginger
2 tbls dark brown sugar
1 tbls garlic powder
1 tbls onion powder
1 tbls kosher salt
2 tsps cayenne pepper
2tsps freshly ground black pepper
2 tsps dried leaf thyme
1 tsp ground cinnamon
1 tsp five spice powder

Place all the ingredients in an airtight container. Put the lid on and shake well until well mixed. Will keep in an airtight container for up to 6 months.

Southwestern Rub

2 ½ tbls chili powder
1 tbls kosher salt
1 tbls freshly ground black pepper
1 tbls ground cumin
1 tbls garlic powder
1 tsp cayenne pepper

Place all the ingredients in an airtight container. Put the lid on and shake well until well mixed. Will keep in an airtight container for up to 6 months.

Texas Rub

3 tbls sweet paprika
3 tbls brown sugar
1 tbls kosher salt
1 tsp ground cumin
1 tsp ground cinnamon

Place all the ingredients in an airtight container. Put the lid on and shake well until well mixed. Will keep in an airtight container for up to 6 months.

Kansas City Rub

2 tbls paprika
1 tbls brown sugar
1 tsp garlic powder
1 tsp freshly ground black pepper
1 tsp kosher salt

Place all the ingredients in an airtight container. Put the lid on and shake well until ewll mixed. Will keep in an airtight container for up to 6 months.

Italian Seasoning

1 tbls dried leaf oregano
1 tbls dried leaf thyme
1 tbls dried leaf basil
1 tsp coarse sea salt
½ tsp crushed red pepper flakes
½ tsp freshly ground lack pepper

Place all the ingredients in an airtight container. Put the lid on and shake well until well mixed. Will keep in an airtight container for up to 6 months.

Sauces

Putting sauce on food is an inexpensive way to compliment food. Whether or not food has been seasoned, marinated or not, a sauce can be just the thing. For example, the Italians dress pasta, which has only been seasoned with salt. This allows the pasta to be the major taste, and the sauce is just a compliment. On the other side, Jamaican Jerk Chicken, which has been seasoned and marinated, tastes twice as good with a barbecue sauce. You decide.

Horseradish Sauce

My Southwest Florida Barbecue Sauce

Chinese Hot Mustard Sauce

Asian Dipping Sauce

Peach Habanero Hot Sauce

Peach Yogurt Sauce

Duck Sauce

Caribbean Barbecue Sauce

Caribbean Chile Sauce

Lemon Butter Sauce

Garlic Butter Sauce

Horseradish Sauce

4 tbls prepared horseradish (see footnote)
½ cup heavy cream
½ cup mayonnaise
½ tsp freshly ground black pepper (optional)

In a medium bowl, mix all the ingredients. Use immediately or store in an airtight container for up to 24 hours.

Footnote. Commercially available prepared horseradish and horseradish sauces are filled with chemicals and fillers, and mask the true flavor of horseradish root. Preparing you own is simple and inexpensive, and can be stored in an airtight container for up to one week.

To prepare your own, simply grate as much of the horseradish root that you need. Mix in white vinegar until you reach the consistency that you like. You can use it right away, or let the flavors marry for up to 3 hours in the refrigerator.

My Southwest Florida Barbecue Sauce

Southwest Florida is not known for barbecue, but I am. After you try this sauce on ribs, chicken, or pork, maybe you will be, also!

2 tbls extra virgin olive oil (evoo)
2 cups ketchup
½ cup chopped yellow onions
¼ cup dark corn syrup
2 tbls fresh lemon juice
2 tbls Dijon mustard
2 tbls dark brown sugar
3 cloves chopped garlic
2 chopped jalapeno chiles
1 tbls Worcestershire sauce
1 tsp hot sauce
1 tsp kosher salt
1 tsp liquid smoke
½ tsp cayenne pepper

1. In a non-reactive saucepan, heat the olive oil over medium-high until smoking. Add the onions and sauté 6-8 minutes. Add the garlic and the chiles and sauté 2-3 minutes more.
2. Add the remaining ingredients and bring to a gentle boil. Reduce the heat and simmer for 20-30 minutes until slightly thickened.

Sauce can be refrigerated in an airtight container for up to 5 days, or up to one month in the freezer.

Chinese Hot Mustard Sauce

This is another example of the commercially available sauces that are full of chemicals and preservatives. This recipe is less expensive without the chemicals.

1/3 cup Chinese hot mustard powder
¼ cup water
3 tbls rice vinegar
pinch of kosher salt

Put the mustard powder in a small bowl and whisk in the water until you have a thin paste. Add the vinegar and salt and whisk well to blend.

Sauce can be refrigerated in an airtight container for up to 5 days.

Asian Dipping Sauce

¼ cup grated carrots
one 1 inch piece of ginger, peeled and chopped
2 cloves chopped garlic
2 tbls evoo
2 tbls rice vinegar
2 tbls soy sauce
1 tbls fish sauce
1 scallion, (green onion) thinly sliced
¼ cup water

1. Heat the oil in a heavy bottomed saucepan over medium-high heat until smoking. Add the garlic and ginger and sauté for 2 minutes, constantly stirring.
2. Add the oil, rice vinegar, soy sauce, fish sauce and the water. Bring to a boil. Reduce the heat and simmer covered for 8-10 minutes. Remove from the heat and add the scallions.

Sauce can be kept in an airtight container for up to one week, but do not freeze.

Peach Habanero Hot Sauce

The sweetness of the peaches and the heat and fruitiness of the chile make for one kicked up flavor. This sauce is great on any chicken. If you think the habanero chile is too hot, substitute what you like, but use half of the honey.

2 tbls evoo
1 small onion, chopped
2 cloves garlic, chopped
3-4 ripe peaches, peeled, pitted, and coarsely chopped
1 tbls honey
1 cup white wine vinegar
kosher salt and freshly ground black pepper

1. Heat the oil in a medium saucepot over medium heat until smoking. Add the onion and garlic. Cook, stirring often until soft, 6-8 minutes. Do not brown. Add the peaches and the chiles and cook, stirring often for ten minutes. Add the honey and the vinegar, reduce the heat, and simmer until slightly thickened, 15-20 minutes.
2. Remove from the heat, and when cool, transfer to a food processor or blender, and blend until smooth. Season with the salt, pepper, vinegar and honey.

Sauce can be refrigerated in an airtight container for up to 5 days, or in the freezer for up to 2 weeks.

Peach Yogurt Sauce

This is a great sauce to use if you think that you may have used too many chile peppers in a marinade. This sauce even mellows out a habanero.

2 or 3 ripe peaches, pitted and diced
2 cups thick yogurt (see footnote)
3 scallions, thinly sliced
kosher salt and freshly ground black pepper

Put the yogurt in a medium bowl and fold in the peaches and the scallions. Season with salt and pepper to taste. Use immediately, or refrigerate in an airtight container for up to 48 hours.

Footnote: To make the thick yogurt, use a yogurt with as much fat content as you can find. Fat free yogurt will not thicken.

1. Line a strainer with paper towels or cheesecloth.
2. Place the strainer in a large bowl.
3. Spoon the yogurt onto the paper towel and refrigerate for 4 hours.
4. Remove the yogurt from the refrigerator and discard the water in the bowl.

Duck Sauce

No. Duck sauce is not made with ducks. The main ingredient is apricots. This is yet another example of fresh versus commercially sold is better.

1 can apricots in syrup
½ cup rice wine vinegar
1 tsp cornstarch solution (see footnote)
Kosher salt

1. Place the apricots and the syrup in a food processor or blender and pulse until coarsely chopped.
2. In a heavy saucepot, add the apricot mixture and the vinegar to a boil. Reduce the heat and stir in the cornstarch solution.
3. Return to a boil and then reduce the heat. (You wont know how thick it will get until you bring the mixture back to a boil.)Simmer until slightly thickened. Let cool.

Footnote: Cornstarch solution is 1 part cornstarch and 2 parts water. Place the water in a small bowl and gradually whisk in the cornstarch until the cornstarch is completely dissolved.

Sauce can be refrigerated in an airtight container for up to 1 week, or stored in the freezer for up to 1 month.

Caribbean Barbecue Sauce

This sauce was created for Jerk chicken, but I like it on a lot of things. Try it-you'll like it.

1 cup freshly squeezed orange juice-3-4 oranges + the zest of one
1 cup granulated sugar
½ cup red wine vinegar
½ cup white wine vinegar
1 yellow onion, chopped
6 cloves garlic, chopped
1 jalapeno, seeded and chopped
1 ½ cups kechup
2 tbls evoo
2 tbls molasses
2 tbls chili powder
2 tbls Dijon mustard
1 tbls brown sugar
1 tbls Worcestershire sauce
kosher salt and freshly ground pepper

1. Combine the orange juice, the red wine vinegar, the white wine vinegar and the sugar in non-reactive saucepan. And boil until reduced to 1 cup. Remove from the heat, add the orange zest, and set aside.
2. In another saucepan, heat the oil over medium-high heat until smoking. Add the onions, garlic and jalapeno and sauté until soft. 5-6 minutes. Add the remaining ingredients and bring to a boil. Reduce the heat and simmer for 20-25 minutes.
3. When the sauce is cool, transfer to a food processor or blender, and blend until smooth.

Sauce can be refrigerated in an airtight container for up to 5 days, or up to one month in the freezer.

Caribbean Chile Sauce

This sauce is a three-alarm fire! If you think that it might be too hot, use a jalapeno instead of the habanero.

¼ cup chopped red onion
4 cloves garlic, chopped
2 inch piece fresh ginger, peeled and chopped
1 habanero chile, seeded and finely chopped
½ cup rice wine vinegar
3 tbls chopped fresh cilantro
2 tbls evoo
2 tbls chopped fresh thyme
2 tbls brown sugar
1 tbls fresh lime juice
1 tbls soy sauce
½ tsp ground allspice
Kosher salt and freshly ground black pepper

1. Heat the oil in a medium saucepot over medium heat until smoking. Add the onions and sauté until soft, 6-8 minutes. Add the garlic, ginger and jalapeno and sauté for 2 minutes, stirring constantly.
2. Add the rest of the ingredients and bring to a boil. Reduce the heat and simmer until thickened, 10-12 minutes.

Sauce can be refrigerated in an airtight container for up to 5 days, or up to one month in the freezer.

Lemon Butter Sauce

This sauce is great for vegetables, fish and chicken. Add the chopped fresh basil, and it's perfect for homemade basil ravioli (page 82).

4 tbls (1/2 stick) unsalted butter
4 tbls evoo
juice and zest of 1 lemon
¼ cup chopped fresh basil leaves (see footnote)
Kosher salt and freshly ground black pepper

1. Heat the oil in a 12 inch sauté pan over medium-high heat until smoking. Add the lemon zest until fragrant, 1-2 minutes.
2. Add the butter and lemon juice. Stir until butter is completely melted, and sauce is slightly thickened. Season with the salt and pepper, remove from the heat, add the basil, and serve with your favorite pasta dish.

Garlic Butter Sauce

This sauce is great on pastas, gnocchi and green vegetables.

2 sticks unsalted butter
2 cloves garlic, minced
½ tsp salt
¼ tsp freshly ground black pepper

In a small saucepot melt the butter on medium-high heat. Add the garlic and sauté, stirring constantly, 3-4 minutes. Remove from the heat and season with the salt and pepper. Serve immediately.

Waste Not-Want Not

Ever wonder what to do with over ripe fruits and vegetables? Stale bread? Chicken bones? I hate wasting food, and I'm sure you do to. Hear are a few ideas that save food and money.

Bread Crumbs

Croutons

S.O.T. Save our Tomatoes

Mystery Sauce

Let's Clean the Garbage Disposal

Chicken Stock

Shrimp/Fish Stock

Bread Crumbs

Cut 2 or 3 day old bread into cubes. Place the cubes in a food processor of blender and pulse to your desired texture. Place the breadcrumbs in an airtight container and put in the freezer until needed. You can season the breadcrumbs before placing them in the freezer, or when you are going to use them.

Croutons

Day old bread, cut into cubes
Extra virgin olive oil
Kosher salt and freshly ground pepper

1. Preheat the oven to 400 degrees.
2. Place the bread cubes on a baking sheet. Drizzle with the olive oil and sprinkle with the salt and pepper.
3. Bake for 15 minutes. Let cool completely before serving.

S.O.T. Save Our Tomatoes

Overripe tomatoes have a tremendous amount of flavor, but the texture makes in difficult to cut and eat. Boil the tomatoes in salted water for 20-30 minutes, or until the skins are falling off. Let cool completely. Peel the skins off and use for sauces instead of using new tomatoes. The tomatoes can be frozen for up to 1 month.

Mystery Sauce

5 or 6 pieces of overripe fruit, diced
1 jalapeno seeded and finely chopped
1 cup of thick yogurt (page 19)
Kosher salt and freshly ground pepper

Place the fruit, the chile, and the yogurt into a food processor or blender and puree. Season the mixture with the salt and pepper. Use this sauce for chicken, pork and vegetables.

Let's Clean the Garbage Disposal

I may be crazy, but have you ever noticed that citrus fruit goes bad overnight? Open the crisper drawer one day and it's perfect. The next day it's rotten. But, it still smells great. For centuries, mankind has known that citrus juice is an exceptional cleaner. It's only recently that cleaning product manufacturers have realized this. Instead of buying artificially produced citrus balls that are full of chemicals and pollutants, send your rotten citrus down the garbage disposal. It should make your kitchen smell like a lemon grove for a while, as well as cleaning the disposal.

Chicken Stock

There are only 2 commercially available chicken stocks that are chemical free and all natural, and naturally, they are more expensive. You might have realized by now, I am not a chemical fan. I also don't like waste. Making your own stocks is the perfect answer. I always have some in the freezer, and I use it instead of water, for soups, sauces, stews, and for braising.

4 lbs. Chicken bones, necks, and wink tips
2 large onions peeled and quartered
2 celery stalks with the leaves cut into 4 pieces each
2 large carrots cut in half
1 head of garlic cut in half
4 bay leaves
1 tbls kosher salt
1 tsp whole black peppercorns
1 tsp dried leaf thyme
1 tsp dried rosemary
1 tsp dried leaf oregano

1. Put all the ingredients in a large stockpot or Dutch oven. Add enough cold water to cover by one inch. Over high heat, bring to a boil. Reduce the heat and simmer for 2-3 hours, skimming off the foam that floats to the top.
2. When cool, place a strainer lined with paper towel over a large bowl. Strain the contents of the pot saving only the liquid.

The stock can be refrigerated for up to 3 days or frozen for up to 2 months.

Shrimp Stock

Shrimp stock is another stock you can use for soups or for braising. This is a delicious way to get something out of shrimp shells, other than the shrimp.

1 lb. shrimp shells and heads
1 small onion, peeled and quartered
1 stalk celery, with leaves, cut into 4 pieces
1 carrot cut into 4 pieces
3 garlic cloves, thinly sliced
3 bay leaves
2 tsp kosher salt
1 tsp whole black peppercorns

1. Put all the ingredients in a large stockpot or Dutch oven. Add enough cold water to cover by one inch. Over high heat, bring to a boil. Reduce the heat and simmer for 2 hours.
2. When cool, place a strainer lined with paper towel over a large bowl. Strain the contents of the pot saving only the liquid.

The stock can be refrigerated for up to 2 days or frozen for up to 1 month.

Appetizers and Salads

Appetizers are supposed to be part of a complete and balanced meal that leaves everyone at the table full. In good economic times shrimp, stuffed quahaugs, and lobster cocktails are common. In lean times, we still need to eat and get full, but we need to be more creative, using leftover chicken and steak in a variety of tasty ways. Most of these recipes could easily become a main course or tomorrows lunch.

Asian Egg Rolls

Charlotte Style Chicken Wings

Summer Chicken and Tomato Stack Salad

Tomato, Cucumber and Onion Salad

Grilled Pineapple and Chicken Salad

Auntie Antoinette's Artichoke Balls

Asian Egg Rolls

Ah-So. What does that mean? Everyone who tries these egg rolls say they are the best they have ever had. And they should be. They're made with fresh ingredients without chemicals or preservatives. This recipe is time consuming. What I do is make a double batch and freeze half for another day. Serve these with sweet and sour chicken, (page 53) and you have a filling Chinese dinner without all the containers.

1 tbls corn starch + 137 pounds for dusting (you'll see)
2 tbls soy sauce
1 lb ground pork
2 tbls vegetable oil + more for deep frying
1 tsp kosher salt
½ tsp cayenne pepper
1 cup scallions, thinly sliced
¾ lb. bok choy, outer leaves removed, cut into matchsticks
½ cup grated carrots
2 tsp garlic, minced
2 tsp ginger, minced (optional)
¼ cup fresh cilantro leaves, chopped
1 tbls asian sesame oil
20 8" all purpose pasta sheets

1. Put the soy sauce in a small bowl and slowly whisk in 1 tbls corn starch
2. Heat 2 tbls oil in a deep skillet over medium high heat. Add the pork, salt, and the cayenne and stir fry until the pork turns pale, 8-10 minutes. Add the bok choy until it begins to soften, 4-5 minutes.Add the scallions, carrots, garlic, ginger, cilantro and sesame oil, and continue stir frying 5-6 minutes. Add the soy sauce mixture and stir well to blend. Bring to a boil for 1 minute and turn off the heat. Keep stir frying 4-5 minutes more. (At this point, you might want to quit and make the egg rolls tomorrow. I've done that. If not, march on.

3. Place a small bowl of water near your work surface. Place a pasta wrapper on your work surface with one of the points pointing at you. Using your finger, wet the edges of the sheet with water. Put a tbls of the pork mixture just below the center of the sheet above the bottom point. Pull the bottom of the wrap up over the filling. Fold in the sides over the filling and roll forward to completely enclose the filling. Wet the seam with more water. Place the egg roll on a baking sheet dusted with corn starch and dust the top of the roll. Continue with the rest of the filling.
4. Preheat the oven to 200 degrees. In a large pot, pour enough oil to fill halfway. Heat the oil to 375 degrees.
5. Carefully place 4-5 egg rolls into the pot. Don't over crowd. Fry until golden brown on all sides. Remove and drain on paper towels and place in the oven until you finish frying.
6. Serve hot with the Chinese mustard sauce and Asian dipping sauce (page 18), and duck sauce. (page 21)

Note: If you made a double batch, wrap the second half in aluminum foil. Place them in airtight containers and freeze them for up to 2 weeks.

Charlotte Style Barbecue Chicken Wings

In 1995, I was fortunate enough to live in Charlotte and work at a racing school. Charlotte is home of both Nascar and great barbecue. As with all good cooks, everyone does it differently. This recipe, which drumsticks or legs can be substituted, gives Texas barbecue a run for its money.

24 chicken wings, legs, or 12 thighs
2 cups apple cider vinegar
1 cup ketchup
4 tbls brown sugar
1 tbls vegetable oil
1 tbls Worcestershire sauce
1 tbls cayenne pepper
½ tbls salt

1. Mix all the ingredients, except the chicken, in a large stockpot and bring to a boil. Add the wings until just cooked through. 20-25 minutes for wings and legs, 30-35 minutes for thighs.
2. When cool, transfer the chicken to a bowl.
3. Heat your grill to high (page 9). Cook 8-10 minutes or until nicely charred, turning and basting with the sauce.

Note: The chicken can also be finished in the oven at 350 degrees for 12-14 minutes.

Summer Chicken and Tomato Stack Salad

This is a great salad that's a meal in itself. Makes a great picnic item, and uses leftover chicken.

For the salad:

½ red onion, thinly sliced
½ cup fresh basil, thinly sliced
5 sprigs fresh Italian flat-leaf parsley
4 tomatoes, thinly sliced
10-12 ounces leftover chicken, torn from the bones
½ cup crumbled goat, feta, or blue cheese

For the dressing:

2 tbls white wine vinegar
1/3 cup evoo
½ tsp dried leaf oregano
½ tsp dried leaf thyme
½ tsp dried basil
Kosher salt and freshly ground pepper

1. Put the vinegar in a bowl and slowly whisk in the oil. Add the remaining ingredients and stir well. Season with salt and pepper.
2. In another bowl, combine the chicken, basil, parsley, onions and the cheese.
3. Place some tomato slices individually on a serving platter. Spoon the chicken mixture onto the tomatoes. Place another tomato slice on top of the salad. Drizzle with the dressing and serve immediately.

Cucumber, Tomato, and Onion Slices

Growing up, we always had fresh tomatoes. My grandmother, mother, and aunts and uncles, all grew tomatoes that we picked when we wanted. With that many tomatoes, there was great opportunity to serve them in a bunch of ways. One of my favorites to this day is thick sliced and drizzled with extra virgin olive oil and sprinkled with dried leaf oregano.

Three tomatoes, cut into 1 inch slices
1 cucumber cut into 1 inch slices
½ red onion cut into 1/8 inch slices
2 tbls evoo
½ tsp dried leaf oregano
pinch of kosher salt

Arrange the vegetable slices on a serving platter, tomato, cucumber and onion. Drizzle with the evoo and sprinkle with the oregano. Serve immediately.

Grilled Pineapple and Chicken Salad

This recipe is a great salad for a hot summer night and makes a great appetizer. Wait until pineapples are in season because they are much sweeter and less expensive, and this is another tasty way to use left over chicken.

10-12 ounces cooked chicken, torn from the bones
1 medium to large pineapple, peeled, cored, and cut into ½ inch rings
1 tbls fresh chopped cilantro
½ cup chopped onions
1 cup salad greens
1 large tomato, cut into wedges
2 tbls evoo
¼ cup red wine vinegar
Kosher salt and freshly ground black pepper

1. Heat your grill to high (page 9), or light your broiler.
2. While the grill is heating put the vinegar in a small bowl, and slowly whisk in the oil. Add the cilantro and season with the salt and pepper.
3. Mix the salad greens, tomatoes, onions and the chicken in a bowl, and set aside.
4. Brush the pineapple slices with oil and season with the salt and pepper. Grill until slightly charred on both sides, 2-3 minutes per side.
5. Place the salad mixture on a serving platter, and place the pineapple slices around the salad. Drizzle with the dressing and serve.

Auntie Antoinette's Artichoke Balls

This is another delicious and inexpensive recipe from another great family cook.

1 15 ounce can artichoke hearts, drained and chopped
¼ cup butter
1 small red onion, finely chopped
2 cloves garlic, finely chopped
½ cup grated parmesan cheese
½ cup bread crumbs, toasted (see footnote)
½ tsp kosher salt

1. In a medium saucepan on medium heat, melt the butter. Do not brown. Add the onions and sauté 6-8 minutes. Add the garlic and the artichokes and cook 2 minutes more.
2. Remove from the heat and add the cheese, salt and bread crumbs, and let the mixture cool.
3. Preheat your oven to 300 degrees. Form the artichoke mixture into bite sized balls. 3-4 dozen.
4. Bake 8-10 minutes and serve hot.

Footnote: To toast bread crumbs, make the bread crumbs (page 26). Heat a. sauté pan and sauté the bread crumbs moving constantly until they are golden brown.

Beef and Pork

My favorites. There are thousands of ways to prepare and cook beef and pork. I've included these recipes because not only do I love beef and pork, I also love barbecue. In this economy, I still want plenty of both, but I still need to save money.

Rib Stickin' Burgers

Southwestern Scrambled Eggs- Your Way

Marinated Top Sirloin with Homemade Horseradish Sauce

Texas Smoked Barbecued Pork Ribs

Grilled Pork Steaks

Dad's Hot Dogs, Beans and Brown Bread

Rhode Island Style Hot Wieners

Barbecued Meat Loaf

Beef Stroganoff

In The House Barbecued Ribs

Rib Stickin Burgers

This recipe is hot. If you think it's to hot, use ½ the jalapeno chiles, or add a tablespoon of honey. Try to use 70% lean beef, because fat matters.

2 lbs ground beef
1/3 cup scallions, green and white parts, chopped
4 jalapeno chiles, seeded and chopped
1 tbls chile powder
1 tbls evoo
kosher salt and freshly ground black pepper

1. In a large bowl using your hands, combine the beef, scallions, chiles and chile powder and mix well. Shape the mixture into 1 inch thick patties.
2. Heat your grill to high (page 9) or light your broiler.
3. Brush the patties with the oil and season with the salt and pepper. Grill the patties for 8 minutes for medium rare, flipping once. 10-12 minutes for medium.

Southwestern Scrambled Eggs-Your Way

If you're like most cooks, you always looking for new ways to prepare eggs. If you're like me, you always looking for ways to use leftovers and save money. I had a similar egg dish in Arizona. It was the first time I had a chile pepper in my eggs. I had heard of hot sauce on eggs, but never a chile pepper.

8 large eggs, beaten
1 cup sharp cheddar cheese, grated
¼ cup chopped fresh cilantro
1 tbls finely chopped jalapeno pepper
3 tbls evoo
1 lb. leftover meat of your choice, chopped

1. In a medium bowl, beat the eggs. Add the cheese, cilantro, jalapeno and the meat, and mix well.
2. Heat the oil in a large skillet, preferably cast iron, on medium high heat until smoking. Pour the egg mixture into the pan and stir constantly until you reach your desired consistency. Serve immediately.

Marinated Top Sirloin with Horseradish Sauce

Let's face it. Top Sirloin has great flavor, but who can chew it? That's why we marinate for up to 24 hours. Not only does that tenderize the meat, it adds bigger flavor. Serve this with the prepared horseradish sauce, page 16, and it is fit for a Texas Cattleman.

2-3 lb piece of top sirloin cut in half
1 cup dry white wine
½ cup brown sugar
2 tbls Chef Lagasses Creole seasoning (page 11)
2 tbls minced garlic
1 tsp freshly ground black pepper
1 recipe prepared horseradish sauce (page 14)

1. In a medium bowl, combine all the ingredients except the steak. Stir well.
2. Place the steaks in a large re-sealable freezer bag. Pour in the marinade and seal the bag, pushing out the air. Roll the steaks around to cover. Refrigerate at least 4 hours, but overnight is better.
3. When ready to cook, heat your grill to high (page 9) or light your broiler. Remove the steak from the marinade. Discard the marinade and pat dry the steaks. Brush the steaks with oil and season with the Creole seasoning. Grill the steaks for 8-10 minutes for rare, turning once. 6-8 minutes more for medium-rare.
4. Remove the steaks to a cutting board and let rest for 10-15 minutes. Cut the steaks diagonally across the grain. Serve with the horseradish sauce.

Note: To cook any large steak in the oven, pre-heat your oven to 350 degrees. In a 12- inch non-reactive sauté pan, heat 2 tablespoons of extra virgin olive oil on high until smoking. Sear the steaks on all 6 sides until nicely charred. Place the whole pan in the oven and cook for 12-15 minutes, turning once.

Texas Smoked Barbecued Pork Ribs

It is said that everything's big in Texas. I don't know about that but Texas barbecue is. It's world famous and full of big flavor. They smoke for days, not just hours. The beans are slow cooked in cast iron over open flames for days, as well. I agree that smoking ribs for 12 hours probably taste's better than if smoked for 2 hours, but I'm not setting my alarm clock every four hours to change coals. They take it serious, and every barbecue cook has his or her own rubs, sauces and techniques. Most people use baby back ribs, but I use plain old pork ribs. They are less expensive and more flavorful, and after they get rubbed, smoked, and basted with sauce, these ribs rock. Serve with My SW Florida barbecue sauce and pass the napkins. This recipe brings Texas barbecue to your house.

2 racks pork ribs
4 tbls Texas rub (page13)
2 cups wood chips
1 cup My SW Florida barbecue sauce (page 17)

1. Remove the ribs from the refrigerator and rub all over with the rub. Let come to room temperature. Soak the wood chips one hour before smoking.
2. Set up your grill according to the directions on pages 6 and 7. When ready, smoke for 2 hours, replacing the wood chips every half hour. In the last half hour, baste with the sauce and turn the racks every 10 minutes.
3. When cool, cut the ribs following the bone line and serve with more sauce.

Grilled Pork Steaks

I love pork steaks. They're full of flavor and inexpensive. You can just cook them in a 12- inch skillet with just olive oil, salt and pepper and finish them in the oven and still get great flavor. See note on page 42. I like to smoke them for that extra flavor.

4 pork steaks
2 tbls Chef Lagasse's Creole seasoning
1 tbls evoo
kosher salt and freshly ground black pepper.

1. Rub the steaks with the Creole seasoning. Wrap in foil and refrigerate for at least 4 hours.
2. When ready to cook, remove the steaks from the refrigerator and let come to room temperature. Heat your grill to high (page 9). Brush the steaks with the oil and season with the salt and pepper. Cook for 12-14 minutes, turning once.

Dad's Hot Dogs, Beans, and Brown Bread

My father was a hard working Police Officer who preferred to eat simply. He worked 60-70 hours a week for us, and this was his favorite Saturday night dinner.

8 hot dogs and rolls
1 cup chicken stock (page 28)
1 12 oz. bottle of beer
1 can of brown bread
1 recipe Mom and Pam's "Old Settlers Beans" (page 71)
1 stick of butter, sliced into 1/8 inch pats

1. Preheat the oven to 400 degrees.
2. In a large saucepot over medium high heat, bring the chicken stock and the beer to a rolling boil.
3. Slice the cornbread into ½ inch slices and place on a greased sheet pan. Place butter pats on the slices and put in the oven for 12-14 minutes.
4. Pre heat a 12-skillet or sauté pan. Butter the sides of the rolls and toast on each side. Place the hot dogs in the beer mixture and boil for 8-10 minutes.
5. In another pot heat the beans.
6. Remove the brown bread from the oven and serve dinner hot with your favorite condiments.

Rhode Island Style Hot Wieners

I moved to Florida 5 years ago. Besides my relatives and friends, I miss the food. That's why I became a cook. Rhode Island, Boston, and New York City have the best Italian food, and the seafood was swimming hours before it's served. Some foods are traditional. Pizza on Federal Hill is the best anywhere. Seafood and steaks are served in every restaurant, and to stay in business, you have to serve good food. Del's Frozen Lemonade and Hot Weiners will be available forever. This recipe is my take, and probably not exact.

8 hot dogs and rolls
1lb ground beef
1 cup sweet onions, chopped
2 tbls evoo
2 tbls paprika
2 tbls chile powder
½ tsp curry
½ tsp allspice
1 tsp kosher salt
¼ tsp cinnamon
yellow mustard to taste
chopped onions to taste
celery salt to taste

1. In a large skillet or sauté pan on medium low, heat the oil. Sweat the onions until soft, not browned. Add the ground beef, paprika, chile powder, curry and allspice. Cook slowly stirring often until the beef is completely floating in the sauce. You might need to add a little water. Add the salt and cinnamon and stir. Remove from the heat.
2. In a medium stock pot, bring water to a boil. Add the hot dogs. Place a strainer over the pot and place the buns in the strainer. RI wieners are famous for this part.
3. When the rolls are steamed and the dogs are cooked, serve immediately.

Barbecued Meatloaf

In case you haven't noticed, I love barbecue. Not only is barbecued food delicious, you can use less expensive beef and pork, and still get big flavors. Meatloaf is meatloaf, unless you kick it up. That's what this is. Kicked up meatloaf that tastes like Texas barbecue.

2 lbs ground beef
1 medium yellow onion, finely chopped
4 cloves garlic, finely chopped
2 eggs, beaten
2 cups bread crumbs (page 26)
1 cup My SW FL barbecue sauce and some for brushing (page 17)
2 tbls chopped fresh parsley
2 tbls Texas Rub (page 13)
1 tbls evoo
1 tbls kosher salt
1 tsp freshly ground black pepper

1. Preheat the oven to 350 degrees, and oil the bottom of a baking dish or ovenproof pan.
2. In a large bowl, combine all the ingredients and mix with your hands. Shape the mixture into a loaf and place it in your baking dish. Brush some sauce over the top. Bake for 90 minutes. Serve hot.

Beef Stroganoff

This recipe is a classic. It's also expensive. Using a lesser quality meat and a meat mallet, you can enjoy it for a fraction of the cost. Use the least expensive beef you can find, and ask your butcher to slice it thin across the grain for you.

1½ lbs beef, thinly sliced
2 tbls evoo
1 medium onion, finely chopped
½ pound sliced mushrooms
2tbls Chef Lagasse's Creole seasoning (page 12)
1 tbls all purpose flour
1 tbls kosher salt
½ cup sour cream
½ cup chicken stock (page 28)
1 16 oz. package egg noodles.

1. Cut the beef slices into 2 inch pieces. Season with the Creole seasoning and set aside.
2. In a large stockpot, bring 6 quarts of water to a boil. Add the egg noodles and salt, and cook to package directions.
3. In a 12 skillet or sauté pan, heat 1 tablespoon of the oil over medium high heat until smoking. Add the beef and stir-fry for 3-4 minutes until lightly browned. Pour the meat and the oil in a medium bowl and set aside.
4. In the same pan, heat the other tablespoon of oil to smoking. Add the onions and cook 2-3 minutes, stirring. Add the mushrooms and chicken stock and cook 2 minutes more. Stir in the flour until blended. Return the meat and it's drippings to the pan. Strain the egg noodles and add them and the sour cream to the pan. Remove from the heat and fold in the egg noodles and serve hot.

In the House Barbecued Ribs

I decided to include this recipe at the last minute for those of you who love barbecue, but don't have a grill or smoker. You can achieve barbecue flavor using your broiler and a big pot of water. If you have an indoor smoker, after you boil the ribs, smoke them for 40 minutes before final preparation.

4 lbs country style pork ribs
2 medium sized yellow onions, cut into quarters
½ cup My SW FL barbecue Sauce (page 17)
2 tbls + 2 tsps Chef Lagasses Creole seasoning
1tbls kosher salt

1. Place the ribs, onions and 2 tbls of the Creole Seasoning in a large stockpot or dutch oven. Fill the pot with enough water to cover. Over high heat, bring to a boil. Reduce the heat to low, and simmer covered for 90 minutes.
2. Remove the ribs from the pot, let cool and pat dry.
3. Preheat your broiler. Places the ribs on a baking pan with a rack, and sprinkle with 2 teaspoons of the Creole seasoning, and brush with the sauce. Put the ribs in the oven 6 inches from the burner. Cook for 20 minutes, turning and basting often.

Chicken

I didn't like chicken until I was in my twenties. My family never knew this, because when chicken was served, I never said a word. I ate whatever else was on the table, and left the chicken alone. Today, I love chicken and search for ways to cook it differently. Chicken is great because no matter how you season and marinate it, its true flavor isn't lost, but enhanced. However you flavor chicken, that's what you get. For example, if you use garlic, you get garlic chicken. If you use butter and lemon, that's what you get. See what I mean? That's why chicken is a great food in a bad economy. Also, please read the chicken warning on page 6.

Caribbean Jerk Chicken

Sweet and Sour Chicken

Smoked Barbecued Chicken

Sunday Roast Chicken

Herb Roasted Chicken

Classic Chicken Parmesan

Chicken Francaise

Lemon Butter Chicken

Creole Chicken Stew

Braised Chicken Thighs

Caribbean Jerk Chicken

Some of the tastiest food I've ever had was in the Caribbean. If you like full big chicken flavor, you'll love this recipe. Use the least expensive fresh chicken you can find, any parts work.

4 lbs chicken parts
½ cup chopped onions
½ cup chopped scallions, green and white parts
¼ cup Caribbean Chili Sauce (page 23)
¼ cup fresh lime juice
1 cup Caribbean Barbecue Sauce (Page 22)
¼ cup orange juice
¼ cup chopped fresh Cilantro
2 tbls brown sugar
2 tbls dried rosemary
2 tbls dried basil
2 tbls dried thyme
2 tbls Dijon mustard
1 tbls allspice
1 tsp Kosher salt

1. Place the chicken in a large re-sealable freezer bag. In a large bowl, mix all the ingredients except the barbecue sauce. Pour the mixture into the bag, and massage the chicken for full coverage. Refrigerate for 1-4 hours.
2. When ready to cook, heat your grill to medium-low.(page 9)
3. Remove the chicken and discard the marinade. Cook until the chicken is falling away from the bone, about 1 hour, turning and basting with the sauce.
4. Let cool 10 minutes and serve.

Note: When marinating with citrus, do not marinate for more than 4 hours. Citrus starts the cooking process and if over marinated, you might end up with dry food.

Sweet and Sour Chicken

You' re family is probably going to tell you that this recipe is not the same as take out. They'll be right! There's no comparison. Contrary to popular belief, Asians don't eat American-Chinese food, and they do not like chemicals and preservatives. This is a time consumer, but it' well worth it.

For the marinade:
2 tbls rice wine vinegar
2 tsp ginger, minced
2/3 tsp kosher salt

For the Sweet and Sour Sauce:
¼ cup rice wine vinegar
¼ cup sugar
6 tbls water
2 tbls corn starch
½ small tomato, diced
½ bell pepper, cut into 1 in squares
2 pineapple rings, cut into bite size pieces
2½ tsp cornstarch solution (page 21)
2 tsp scallion, green and white parts, chopped
1 tsp soy sauce
1 tsp minced ginger
1 tsp oil, heated

For the batter:
¾ lb pork, cit into ¾ in. cubes
¾ cup flour
¼ cup cornstarch
¾ cup water
1 ¼ tsp baking powder
½ tsp sugar
½ tsp oil

1. In a small bowl, mix the marinade. Add the pork, cover, and refrigerate for at least 1 hour.
2. In a medium non-reactive saucepot over medium-high, heat the oil until smoking. Add the ginger and stir for 30 seconds. Add the vinegar, sugar, water and the scallions. Cook for 2 minutes. Reduce the heat to simmer and let sit.
3. In a small bowl, combine the batter ingredients. Coat the pork with the cornstarch and dip in the batter. In a wok or 12 in skillet, heat enough oil to deep fry. In batches, fry the pork until golden brown. Strain on paper towels.
4. Turn the heat under the sweet and sour sauce to medium high. Add the tomato, bell pepper and the pineapple and cook for two minutes. Remove from the heat and add the pork ad the cornstarch solution. Stir well to combine, and serve hot.

Smoked Barbecue Chicken

This recipe and the cooking technique may create the best barbecue chicken you've ever had.

2 3-4 lb chickens cut into quarters
2 cups wood chips
1 cup My SW FL Barbecue Sauce (page 17)
2 tbls Chef Lagasse's Original Creole Seasoning (page 12)

1. Place the chicken parts on a large platter and rub both sides with the seasoning. Cover and refrigerate from 4-24 hours.
2. 2 hours before cooking, soak the wood chips. 1 hour before cooking, allow the chicken to come to room temperature.
3. Heat your grill or prepare your hardwood charcoal for a low fire. Pages 7,8 and 9.
4. Arrange the chickens on the cool side of the grill. Close the lid and smoke for 40 minutes, adding new wood chips every 20 minutes.
5. Remove the chickens from the grill, and place them on two sheets of large aluminum foil. Brush the chickens with the sauce and wrap them tightly.
6. Return to the cool side of the grill and cook 20 minutes more. Serve when ready with more sauce.

Sunday Roast Chicken

This is another delicious chicken dish for a cold Sunday afternoon. This one deserves to have the family altogether.

1 4-5 lb roaster chicken
2 lemons
2 tbls evoo
2 tbls salt
1 tbls freshly ground black pepper

1. Preheat the oven to 375 degrees.
2. In small bowl, whisk together the oil, salt and pepper. Rub the chicken all over with the oil mixture. Squeeze the lemon juice all over the chickens, and place the lemons in the cavity.
3. Place the chicken on a roasting pan or ovenproof dish, breast side up. Cook for 1 ½ to 2 hours, basting with the juices. Let rest for 15 minutes before carving.

Herb Roasted Chicken

I love fresh thyme and fresh rosemary. Either one gives a nice earthy flavor to the chicken. I use rosemary in the winter and thyme in the summer.

4   tbls fresh thyme or rosemary, finely chopped and stems reserved
2 tbls evoo
2 tsp kosher salt
2 tsp freshly ground black pepper

1. Preheat the oven to 425 degrees.
2. Rub the chicken all over with the oil, and sprinkle all sides with the salt and pepper.
3. Sprinkle the chopped herbs all over and place the stems in the cavity.
4. Place the chicken in an ovenproof baking dish or roasting pan. Cook for 1 ¼ to 1 ½ hrs. Let cool for 15 minutes before carving.

Classic Chicken Parmesan

Being Italian, this is probably my all time favorite chicken dishes. Traditionally, chicken breasts are used, but in lean times, I've used thighs. They actually have a deeper, more earthy flavor than the breasts. If using breasts, place them one at a time in a resealable freezer bag, and pound them to an even thickness. This allows for more even cooking.

4 boneless, skinless chicken breast or 6-8 thighs
2 tsps Chef Lagasse's Creole seasoning (page 12)
½ tsp kosher salt
¼ cup all-purpose flour
2 eggs, lightly beaten
¾ cup unseasoned bread crumbs
4 tbls evoo
½ recipe Tomato Sauce My Way (page 79)
½ lb fresh mozzarella, sliced ¼ inch thick (page 78)
1 lb fresh pasta (page 75)
¼ cup grated parmesan cheese

1. Place the flour, egg, and bread crumbs in three separate bowls. Season the chicken with the salt and the seasoning. Dip each piece of chicken in the flour, the eggs, and the bread crumbs, until all are breaded.
2. Heat 2 tablespoons of the olive oil in a large skillet on medium heat. Cook the chicken pieces for 4 minutes on one side, and 2 minutes on the other, adding more oil if needed, and remove from the heat.
3. Place the chicken in a large baking dish lined with the sauce. Spoon ¼ cup of the sauce on each piece. Place mozzarella slices on each piece and sprinkle with the parmesan cheese. .
4. Pre-heat the oven to 350 degrees. Cook the chicken for 15 minutes. Raise the oven to broil and cook until the cheese is bubbling and lightly golden. Serve hot with the fresh pasta.

Chicken Francaise

This is another classic chicken dish that really let's the chicken flavor ring. The white wine and the parsley are optional, but do not substitute any vinegar. You can use chicken cutlets, which are too expensive for my taste, or chicken breasts. In my markets, boneless, skinless are $5.00 a pound on sale. I buy them with the skin and bones, and remove the bones myself.

2 8 ounce chicken breasts
2 eggs, lightly beaten
½ cup white wine
½ cup chicken stock (page 28)
¼ cup fresh lemon juice
2 tbls butter
1 tbls fresh chopped parsley
¼ cup evoo
¼ cup all purpose flour
Kosher salt and freshly ground white pepper

3. Cut the chicken breasts in half. Place 2 pieces in a re-sealable freezer bag and flatten the pieces. Repeat with the other 2.
4. Place the beaten egg and the flour in 2 separate bowls. Dip the pieces in the flour and then the eggs.
5. Heat the oil and the butter over medium heat until the butter is melted. Do not brown. Saute the chicken pieces until golden brown, about 2 minutes each side. Add the lemon juice swirl the pan until the sauce is slightly thickened. Remove from the heat and season with the salt, pepper, and the parsley. Serve immediately.

Lemon Butter Chicken

I love what happens when lemon and butter get married. The flavor the mixture gives fish poultry and vegetables is from another planet. Try this recipe with fish, and see what you think.

4-5 lb roaster chicken
1 stick unsalted butter at room temperature
2 lemons
2 tbls Chef Lagasse's Creole Seasoning

3. Preheat the oven to 350 degrees Place the chicken in an oven-proof baking dish or roasting pan. Rub the butter all over the chicken and season with the Creole Seasoning.
4. Squeeze the juice from the 2 lemons all over the chicken, and place the rinds in the cavity. Cook for 1 ½ to 1 ¾ of an hour. Let rest for 15 minutes before carving.

Creole Chicken Stew

Creole cooking is an art form itself. Louisiana Cooks are as diversified as Italian cooks. The best way to approach Creole cooking is to follow the recipe to the letter.

3-4 pound chicken, cut up
½ cup chopped yellow onions
1 green pepper, diced
1 celery stalk, diced
3 garlic cloves, minced
1 tbls all purpose flour
1 (28) ounce can tomatoes, with the juice
1 lb. okra, cut into ½ inch slices
2 cups chicken stock (page 28)
1 cup long-grain rice
2 tbls evoo
2 tbls Chef Lagasses Creole seasoning (page 12)
1tsp cayenne pepper
Kosher salt and freshly ground black pepper

3. In a large stockpot or Dutch oven, heat the oil over medium high heat until smoking. Season the chicken parts with the Creole seasoning and add the chicken parts. Cook until golden brown, about 2 minutes on each side. Remove to a bowl.
4. In the same pot with the drippings, over medium heat, add the onions, green pepper and the celery and sauté 6-8 minutes. Add the garlic and cook 3-4 minutes more, stirring occasionally.
5. Add the flour, tomatoes, okra, cayenne, salt and pepper, and bring to a boil. Reduce the heat and simmer for 30 minutes, stirring occasionally, until the chicken is falling off the bones.
6. In another saucepot, add the chicken stock and the rice. Cook as the label directs.
7. When ready, place some rice in the bottom of a large soup bowl and add a serving of chicken. Season with the salt and pepper and serve hot.

Braised Chicken Thighs

I love chicken thighs. They have a deeper flavor than breasts, and are less expensive. If you prefer breast, substitute for the thighs.

6 chicken thighs
2 tbls evoo
2 tbls Chef Lagasse's Creole seasoning (page 12)
1 small onion, roughly chopped
2 cloves garlic, chopped
1 large tomato, diced
1 cup chicken stock (page 28)
1 tsp Dijon mustard
Salt and freshly ground pepper

3. Season the thighs with the Creole seasoning. In a 12 skillet or sauté pan on medium high heat, heat the oil until smoking. Add the onion and cook until soft, 6-8 minutes. Add the garlic and cook until fragrant, about 2 minutes. Add the chicken and cook until golden, about 2 minutes on each side.
4. Add the chicken stock, tomatoes, mustard, and season with salt and pepper. Bring to a boil. Reduce the heat, cover, and simmer for 20-25 minutes, until chicken is falling off the bones. Serve hot.

Side Dishes

Side dishes are an important part of any meal. Not only for their nutritional value, but they help to balance out the main course. For example, cole slaw with barbecue. The sweetness of the slaw balances out the heat from the chile peppers in the sauce. Some of these are classics, and others you may never have thought of trying. Until now, that is.

Grilled Potato Stacks

Asian Style Green Beans

Italian Style Green Beans

Grilled Corn on the Cob

Grilled Potatoes

Homemade French Fries

Southwest Style Fries

Mom's and Pam's "Old Settlers Beans"

Pan Toasted Garlic Bread

Green Beans and Tomatoes

Grilled Potato Stacks

This was one of the tomato dishes I grew up on. It was served throughout tomato season at my grandmothers, my house, and every one of my aunt's houses, all with a different spin.

4 lg. baking potatoes, peeled, scrubbed, and cut into ¼ inch slices
4 lg. tomatoes, cut into ¼ inch slices
3 tbls evoo
1 tbls dried oregano
1 tbls dried thyme
1 tbls dried basil
1 cup bread crumbs, (page 26)

3. Heat your grill to high, page 9, or light your broiler.
4. In a small bowl, mix the oregano, thyme, basil and bread crumbs.
5. Place the tomato slices on top of the potato slices and drizzle with the oil. Spread a thin layer of the herb mixture on top of the tomato slices.
6. If using a grill, place the stacks directly on the grate. Close the lid and cook for 10-12 minutes, until the tomatoes are soft. If using a broiler, place a rack on top of an oven pan. Place the stacks on the grate and cook for 8-10 minutes.

Asian Style Green Beans

I love ginger as much as I love garlic, sometimes ever together. This is a simple inexpensive way to dress the beans, but not hide their own flavor. If fresh beans are too expensive, like they are here, substitute frozen or canned, but don't change the cooking time.

1 lb. green beans
2 tbls Asian Sesame Oil or evoo
1 tbls fresh ginger, finely chopped
1 clove garlic, finely chopped

1. Steam the beans if using fresh until your desired tenderness.
2. In a 12 inch skillet or wok, heat the oil on medium high until smoking.
3. Add the ginger and the garlic and stir-fry for 30 seconds. Add the beans and stir fry for 3-4 minutes. Serve hot.

Italian Style Green Beans

There are as many variations of this dish as there are Italian cooks. There is no right or wrong way to prepare beans Italian Style, so use your imagination.

1 lb. green beans
4 cloves garlic, thinly sliced
2 tbls evoo
1 tsp. red pepper flakes
1 tsp Kosher salt

1. In a large skillet or wok, heat the oil over medium high heat until smoking. Add the garlic and cook until fragrant, about 2 minutes.
2. Add the salt and the red pepper. Add the beans, reduce the heat, cover and simmer for 10-12 minutes, until the beans are al dente, until they have a slight crunch. Serve cold.

Grilled Corn on the Cob

You think I'm crazy? I may be, but I thought grilling corn was crazy too, until I did it. However, it is so good, you may never boil corn on the cob again.

8 ears of corn, silks removed and husks reserved
2 tbls evoo
Kosher salt and freshly ground black pepper

1. Pull down enough of the husks to remove the silk, and loosely re-wrap the husks. Holding the corn upright, drizzle the olive oil down the ear of the corn, and season with the salt and pepper.
2. Heat your grill to high (page 9) or light your broiler. Place the corn on the grill and close the lid, or place in the broiler directly on a grate. Cook for 15-20 minutes, turning occasionally. Let cool a little and serve.

Grilled Potatoes

Have you gotten the idea that I love grilling? Of course you have. It's the least expensive way to cook, and it brings out more earthy flavors than other forms of cooking. You won't believe how good potatoes taste grilled.

4 large baking potatoes, scrubbed, peeled and cut into ¼ inch slices
2 tbls evoo
2 tbls chopped fresh parsley
Kosher salt and freshly ground pepper

1. Heat your grill to high (page 9) or light your broiler.
2. Drizzle one side of the potato slices with the oil, and season with the salt and pepper.
3. Place the seasoned side down on the grate and cook 4-6 minutes. Season the top side with the rest of the oil, the salt and the pepper. Flip them over and cook the other side for 3-4 minutes, until nicely charred on both sides. Sprinkle the parsley on the potatoes and cook for 2 more minutes. Serve immediately.

Note: To cook in the broiler, use a grated sheet pan and follow the same directions.

Homemade French Fries

I used to buy frozen fries until the price doubled. Now I buy 5 lb bags of baking potatoes when they are on sale. They'll keep for up to 3 weeks in a cool dry place. The first time I tried fresh potato fries, I couldn't believe the flavor I was missing by eating "fresh frozen" fries.

4 large potatoes scrubbed, peeled and cut into ¼ inch by ¼ inch strips
3- 4 cups vegetable oil
Kosher salt

1. Fill a large stockpot or Dutch oven halfway up the sides with the oil. On medium heat, heat the oil to 360 –370 degrees. You will need a candy thermometer if you don't have a tabletop fryer.
2. In batches to avoid crowding, cook the potatoes for 3-4 minutes to blanch them. Remove to a plate lined with paper towel.
3. When finished with all the fries, again, in batches, cook the fries 3-4 minutes more, until golden brown. Remove from the oil and season with the salt and serve immediately. See footnote.

Footnote: When deep frying anything, you want to season as soon as they come out of the oil The seasoning adds more flavor than if you wait.

Southwest Style Fries

The first time I had these, was in Scottsdale Arizona. I didn't realize it until I visited, but they serve up some fine barbecue that can compete anywhere.

4 baking potatoes, scrubbed, peeled and cut into ¼ in. by 1 inch slices
3-4 cups vegetable oil
2 tbls chile powder
1 tbls kosher salt
1 tsp ground cumin

1. Fill a large stockpot or Dutch oven halfway up the sides with the oil. On medium heat, heat the oil to 360-370 degrees. You will need a candy thermometer if you don't have a tabletop fryer.
2. In batches to avoid crowding, cook the potatoes for 3-4 minutes to blanch them. Remove to a plate lined with paper towel.
3. When finished with all the fries, again, in batches, cook the fries 3-4 minutes more, until golden brown. Remove from the oil and season with the salt and serve immediately.

Mom's and Pam's "Old Settlers Beans"

My Italian mother was a great non-Italian cook. She preferred American food, such as steak and onions, rather than spaghetti and meatballs. She had this recipe and my sister Pamela took it to another level.

½ lb. bacon, chopped
½ lb. ground beef
1 large onion, roughly chopped
½ cup brown sugar
1 cup My SW FL Barbecue Sauce (page 17)
2 tbls Dijon mustard
2 tbls molasses
½ tsp chile powder
1 tsp kosher salt
1 16 oz. can Cannellini beans
1 16 oz. can lima beans
1 16 oz can kidney beans

1. Pre-heat the oven to 350 degrees.
2. In a large stockpot or Dutch oven on medium heat, render the bacon until cooked about halfway. Add the onions and sauté until softened, 6-8 minutes. Add the ground beef, stirring constantly and cook until browned. Add the rest of the ingredients and bring to a boil.
3. Cover the pot and place in the oven and bake for 1hour.

Pan Toasted Garlic Bread

This is an interesting way to toast garlic bread. Probably developed by the French, although it's Italian.

8 slices day old crusty bread
2 tbls evoo
2 tbls butter
4 garlic cloves, cut in half
¼ cup grate parmesan cheese

1. Heat the oil and the butter in a 12 inch sauté pan over medium heat until the butter melts. Do not brown.
2. Place 2 slices of the bread at a time in the pan and brown, 2-3 minutes per side. When browned, rub one side of the bread with a ½ clove of garlic and sprinkle with the cheese. Serve hot.

Green Beans with Tomatoes

This is another classic. Every cook I know makes this dish, but no two are the same. Again, you can use frozen or canned.

1 lb. fresh string beans cut into 1 inch pieces
1 (16 oz) can crushed tomatoes with the juice
2 tbls evoo
2 cloves garlic, thinly sliced
Kosher salt and freshly ground black pepper

1. Heat the oil in a 12inch skillet or sauté pan over medium-high heat until smoking Add the garlic and sauté until fragrant, about 2 minutes.
2. Add the rest of the ingredients and bring to a boil. Lower the heat, cover and simmer for 18-20 minutes. Serve hot or cold.

Italian Specialties

My grandmother, Nonni, came to America from Italy in 1909, bringing with her the art of Italian cooking. Simple fresh ingredients, thoughtful techniques, and the knowledge of the connection between the earth, the sea, food and people. I love barbecue, but there is nothing like the smell of fresh bread in the oven, or a sauce simmering all day, making even the neighborhood smell good.

The art of Italian cooking is more of a concept than that of techniques. Very few ingredients go into most Italian dishes, preserving and enhancing the flavor. Fish, for example, will seldom have more than 5 ingredients. Italian's prefer that their fish was swimming the day they eat it, and want to taste the sea, and not a flavorful sauce.

Italians start eating, drinking, cooking and visiting at the start of day. Dining on breads, cheeses, pastas and fish. They celebrate God, the earth, the sea and people. Anytime of the day, you can enter an Italian home and find fresh food ready to eat. And you better eat. You will hurt an Italian's feelings if you don't. Even if you just ate, you will eat some more.

Italian families eat together daily, and Sunday dinner is a grand affair for all the relatives. Unfortunately, we have lost that in this country. When I was growing up, it was not uncommon for me to have breakfast at my house, brunch at an aunt's house, dinner at another aunt's, and dessert at my grandmothers, or any combination. You get the picture. In Italy today, it's still like that. If you ever get a chance to go, sample as much food as you can. Three cooks can prepare the same dish, with 3 different, delicious results.

Homemade Bread
Fresh Pasta
Spinach Pasta
Gnocchi
Spinach Gnocchi
Fresh Mozzarella Cheese
Ricotta Cheese
Tomato Sauce My Way
Italian Style Meatloaf
Nonni's Calamari
Homemade Basil Ravioli with Lemon and Butter Sauce
Any Old White Fish Will Do
Spaghetti with Garlic and Oil
Homemade Sausage
Florentine Style Bread Soup
Fresh Mozzarella and Basil Bruschetta
Artichoke and Olive Salad
Caprese Salad

Homemade Bread

Bread is a very important food in Italy, and everyone makes their own. This is the best and only way to keep the cost down, and the chemicals out.

6 cups all-purpose flour
1 cup warm water, 105-110 degrees
1 package dry yeast
1 tsp salt
1tsp sugar
1/3 cup evoo

1. Dissolve the yeast in the water to let it proof. You will see and smell when it's ready.
2. On a flat clean work surface, mix the flower, salt and sugar. Make a well, meaning dig out the inside of the flour so your have a round wall of flour and a big hole in the middle. Add the oil and the yeast mixture into the hole. Using a fork, and starting at the bottom of the well, start mixing the flour into the oil and yeast. Add more hot water if necessary, blending thoroughly until the dough has an elastic consistency.
3. Knead the dough until an indention in the dough will spring back, but do not over knead the dough. Place the dough into a large bowl and cover with a clean dish- towel. Let rise in a warm dry place until it doubles in size.
4. Cut the dough in half, and let rise again. When ready, preheat the oven to 375 degrees. Shape the dough into 2 loaves, in the shape of your choice. Place the dough into buttered or oiled baking dishes or on a buttered or oiled baking sheet. Brush some melted butter on the tops of the loaves, and bake for 45 minutes to 1 hour, until golden brown.

Fresh Pasta

Pasta to Italians is probably the most common **food. Dry Pastas are terrific with certain meats and cheeses, but when Italians want a gentle sauce, such as Alfredo, they want fresh Pasta that will let you taste the Pasta. Sauces are to Pasta what dressings are for salads. In this country, the ratio is usually 2 parts sauce to 1 part Pasta. It should be 1 part Pasta and ½ part sauce.**

The Pasta recipes make enough to serve four as a first course, or 2 as a main course. If you have a Pasta machine, follow the manufacturers directions. If not, use a rolling pin and roll it out to the thickness you desire. Left uncut, use it for Ravioli or stuffed Manicotti. For Fettuccine, roll out to ½ inch.

Flavored Pastas

In Italy, Pastas flavored with vegetables and herbs are popular, both in homes and restaurants. You can even find pastas flavored with red wine. To flavor fresh Pasta, chop and puree whatever you're using to a fine powder. Add 3 tablespoons of your mixture for one pound of Pasta. Blend the mixture into the eggs before your mix the flour into the eggs. If the dough is too wet, add a little flour and knead until it holds together.

Fresh Pasta

3 ½ cups all-purpose flour
4 extra-large eggs
½ tsp evoo

1. Pour the flour on a flat clean work surface and make a well, meaning dig out the inside of the flour so your have a round wall of flour and a big hole in the middle. Add the oil and the eggs into the hole. Using a fork, and starting at the bottom of the well, beat the eggs and the oil together and start mixing in the flour. As the mixture starts coming together, keep working the flour from the bottom to retain the well's shape. If the mixture won't stay together, add more flour.
2. When it is altogether, start kneading the dough with both hands. You should have a solid ball. When you do, clean the work surface and re-flour it. Knead the dough for 6-7 more minutes. At this point, it should be a little sticky and spongy.
3. Place the dough in a large bowl and cover with a clean damp dishtowel. Let it rest for 30 minutes in a warm dry place. Roll out the dough into sheets, and cut and shape as desired.

Spinach Pasta

3 ½ cups all-purpose flour
4 extra-large eggs
½ tsp evoo
5 ozs cooked spinach, chopped

Follow the fresh Pasta directions, and add the spinach when you add the eggs and the oil.

Gnocchi

Gnocchi is a delicious variation of Pasta made with potatoes, as well as flour.

3 lbs baking potatoes, scrubbed and peeled
2 cups all-purpose flour
1 egg
1 tsp Kosher or sea salt
½ cup evoo

1. Place the potatoes in a large stockpot and fill the pot with enough water to cover. Bring to a boil, reduce the heat, and simmer for 45-50 minutes. Let cool enough to handle.
2. When cool, run the potatoes through a vegetable mill, or simply mash them. Put the potatoes on a floured work surface and make a well (page 76), and sprinkle the flour over the potatoes.
3. Break the egg into the well and add the oil and the salt. Again, using a fork and starting at the bottom, stir into the wall until the egg is completely mixed in. Gently knead the dough together into a ball, and knead for 4 minutes more.
4. Divide the ball into 4 pieces and make 4 balls. Roll each ball into ropes, approximately ¾ inch thick, and cut the ropes into 1 inch pieces. Using a fork, make an indention into each piece. It should loosely resemble an oyster shell Sprinkle flour onto the pieces and set aside.
5. When ready to cook, bring 4 quarts of water to a boil, and set up an ice bath. In batches to avoid overcrowding, cook the Gnocchi for 1 minute or until they float to the surface. Place the cooked Gnocchi into the ice bath and finish cooking the rest. Remove from the ice bath and in a large bowl, toss the Gnocchi with olive oil. Serve with you favorite Pasta Sauce, or place in an airtight container and refrigerate for up to 2 days.

Spinach Gnocchi

1 ½ lbs baking potatoes
1 ½ lbs cooked spinach
1 ¼ cups all-purpose flour
1 egg
1 tsp Kosher or sea salt
2 tbls evoo

Follow the directions for Gnocchi, and add the spinach when you add the egg, oil and salt.

Fresh Mozzarella Cheese

Mozzarella is a staple in Italian kitchens. It's eaten countless ways, fresh or cooked. I love Mozzarella, but I don't like the price. That's why I've included the recipe.

1 lb Fresh Mozzarella Curd
2 tbls Kosher or sea salt
candy thermometer

1. In a large stockpot or Dutch oven on low heat, bring 6 quarts of water to 120-125 degrees. Place a colander into the water. Crumble the cheese curd into the colander. Using a wooden spoon, stir the curd until it starts to come together
2. Remove the colander from the water and let the cheese cool. Using you hands, gently pull the cheese like you were pulling taffy, but do not over pull. If the cheese hardens too fast, submerge it back in the water and return to pulling. When the cheese feels heavy, it's done. Roll it into balls. Store the cheese in a container of salted water, or wrap them in plastic wrap and refrigerate. Eat within 48 hours.

Ricotta Cheese

Ricotta in Italian means re-cooked. The liquid leftover from the pulling process is a cloudy semi-thick liquid. Ricotta can be used in savory dishes or desserts.

Bring the liquid to a boil. Reduce the heat to low. Stir and simmer until the consistency is similar to small curd cottage cheese.

Tomato Sauce My Way

Traditionally, tomato sauce is fill of spices and herbs, sometimes flavored with yesterdays roast, and simmered for 8-12 hours. That is a Pasta sauce, not a tomato sauce. A Tomato sauce is basically tomatoes simmered for 20-30 minutes, and becomes a component of other dishes. This sauce is just that. It is great on Pasta as is with some parmesan cheese, but it has many other uses.

2 28 oz. cans whole tomatoes
4 cloves garlic, thinly sliced
1 medium red onion, chopped
2 tbls evoo
2 tbls chopped fresh thyme
1 tbls dried oregano
Kosher or sea salt and freshly ground black pepper

1. In a large bowl, crush the tomatoes by hand, with the juice.
2. In a large soup pot or Dutch oven, heat the oil; over medium-high heat until smoking. Add the onions and cook, stirring often, for 6-8 minutes. Add the garlic until fragrant, about 2 minutes. Add the tomatoes, thyme and the oregano and bring to a boil. Reduce the heat and simmer for 20 minutes. Season with the salt and pepper.

Sauce can be kept in an airtight container in the refrigerator for up to 1 week.

Italian Style Meat Loaf

Meat loaf was another dish that when I was growing up was cooked differently by my aunts, mother and grandmother. They did all agree on one thing though. The cheese had to be in there. This is my take on the recipe, but feel free to add Tomato Sauce My Way, (page 79).

1 lb. ground beef
1 lb. ground pork
2 cloves garlic, finely chopped
2 cups bread crumbs (page 26)
¾ cup grated parmesan cheese
4 eggs
1 tsp Kosher or sea salt
½ tsp freshly ground black pepper

1. Preheat the oven to 375 degrees.
2. In a large bowl, using your hands, mix all the ingredients, well.
3. Remove the mixture to a clean work surface and form the mixture into a bread shaped loaf. Place the loaf in an oiled baking dish and bake for 1 hour.

Nonni's Calamari

My grandmother was the greatest cook I've ever known. Her knowledge of cooking could fill 3 cookbooks, before the recipes. She knew exactly how long to cook something. For example, she simmered her sauce for 12 hours, but cooked seafood in minutes. She used basic ingredients, nothing fancy. She said that you had to taste the main ingredient, whatever it was. You can accent it, but never mask it. It would've been a sin if you did. She could also broil a steak and have it turn out delicious. That's why I use a grill, because I can't! This recipe is the perfect balance of the heat from the crushed red pepper and the sweetness of the raisins, and still allowing the calamari to be tasted.

1 cup Risotto
2 ozs. evoo
2 tbls pine nuts
4 cloves garlic, thinly sliced
2 tbls raisins
2 ozs. capers
1 tbls crushed red pepper flakes
2 cups Tomato Sauce My Way (page 79)
4 ozs. dry white wine
½ cup thinly sliced scallions
Kosher or sea salt and freshly ground black pepper
12 ozs. cleaned calamari tubes, cut into ¼ ich rounds, tentacles cut in half

1. In a large stockpot, bring 3-4 quarts of water to a boil. Add the Risotto and 1 tablespoon of salt and cook for 3-4 minutes. Set up an ice bath on your work surface. When the Risotto is cooked, strain it and plunge it into the ice bath.
2. In a 12-14 inch sauté pan or skillet over medium high heat, heat the oil until smoking. Add the garlic, capers and pepper flakes and sauté for 2 minutes. Add the pine nuts and the raisins and cook for 2 minutes more. Add the wine, sauce and the Risotto, and bring to a boil. Add the calamari and stir constantly until the calamari is opaque, 4-5 minutes.
3. Remove from the heat and add 2/3's of the scallions and stir to mix. Pour the mixture into a large bowl and season with salt, pepper, and the rest of the scallions. Drizzle with olive oil and serve hot.

Homemade Basil Ravioli with Lemon and Butter Sauce

Ravioli can be stuffed with anything you like, and it doesn't have to be Italian. There are some very interesting and tasty Southwestern Ravioli floating around. I like this recipe because it is Italian, it's expensive and delicious.

1 recipe fresh pasta dough, (page 76) cut in sheets
16 ozs. Ricotta cheese
¼ cup fresh basil leaves, chopped
1 recipe Lemon Butter Sauce (page 24)
2 tbls + 1 tsp Kosher or sea salt

1. In a large bowl, combine the cheese, basil and the salt, and mix well.
2. Place a fresh Pasta sheet on a clean floured workspace. Using a pastry cutter or the rim of a glass, cut discs out of the Pasta sheet. Place a ½ tsp of the cheese mixture just below the center of the disc. Fold the disc over the mixture so the ends meet. Using a fork, crimp the ends where the Pasta meets. Place on a flour- dusted platter. Continue with the rest of the mixture. Any leftover Pasta dough can be reshaped or cooked as "rags".
3. In a large pot, bring 4 quarts of water to a boil. Add the Ravioli and 2 tablespoons of salt and cook 3-4 minutes, until the Ravioli floats to the top.
4. Place the Lemon Butter sauce in a 12 inch skillet and heat on low. When the Ravioli is done, strain and pour directly into the skillet with the sauce. Toss to coat and serve immediately.

Any Old White Fish Will Do

I didn't pick a fish for this recipe, because as the name says, any fish will do. I use the freshest fish that's on sale. Try to get fish that was never frozen. There is a big taste difference.

6 six oz. fish fillets
½ cup capers
2 tbls evoo
2 tbls unsalted butter
¼ cup chopped fresh parsley
Kosher salt and freshly ground black pepper

1. Season the fish with salt and pepper.
2. In a 12 inch skillet or sauté pan, heat the oil over medium heat until smoking. Add the butter and quickly swirl into the oil. Do not brown. Without over crowding, cook the fillets for 2-3 minutes on the first side. Flip the fish, and add the parsley and the capers.
3. Move the fish to a serving platter and pour the oil-butter sauce over the fish and serve immediately.

Spaghetti Aglio Olio

In Southern Italy, garlic and olive oil are abundant. They're not expensive, either. Here in America, olive oil is pricey, but the amount used most of the time is not enough to worry about the price. I only use extra virgin olive oil in all my cooking, as did my grandmother. You may use a lesser grade olive oil if you prefer, without much of a taste difference.

4 quarts water
2 tbls Kosher or sea salt
1 lb dry spaghetti
6 garlic cloves, thinly sliced
¼ cup evoo
¼ cup grated parmesan cheese
¼ tsp crushed red pepper flakes

1. In a large pot, bring the water to a rolling boil. Add the Spaghetti and salt at the same time. Cook for 7-8 minutes.
2. Meanwhile, in a 12 skillet or sauté pan on medium heat, heat 2 tbls olive oil until smoking. Add the garlic and sauté for 2-3 minutes. Add the rest of the olive oil and reduce the heat to low.
3. When the Spaghetti is done, strain well and pour it into the skillet. Toss the Spaghetti to completely cover. If the sauce seems to dry, add a ¼ cup of the pasta water. Serve hot with the parmesan cheese.

Homemade Sausage

Italian Sausage at the market can be expensive, and sometimes not very good. Italians have made their own sausages for centuries. Try this recipe yourself, and I'm willing to bet you will never buy Italian sausage again. You will need to get sausage casings from your butcher or specialty market. I recommend all natural versus any other.

1 lb freshly ground pork butt
1 tsp crushed red pepper flakes
½ tsp fennel
½ tsp Kosher salt
sausage casings

1. Mix the pork and the spices in a large bowl. Cover and refrigerate for 2 hours.
2. Soak the casings in water for 20 minutes and then rinse them in warm water.
3. Using a long neck funnel, slip one end of the casing over the neck of the funnel and tie tightly. Spoon the pork mixture into the funnel until the casing is full. Twist the casing every few inches at the length you want your sausages and cut at those points.
4. When ready to cook, use a fork to poke holes in the sausages. Sausage can be broiled, baked, fried, or grilled.

Florentine Style Bread Soup

Soups are very common in Italy. Centuries ago they were popular because they are very filling. Today, they probably still are, but Italy isn't as poor as it once was. This is an amazing recipe from my Aunt Antoinette. Serve with crusty garlic bread and you have a meal.

1 16 oz can cannellini beans, drained
1 bunch broccoli, cut into 1 inch pieces
5 cups chicken stock (page 28) or water
4 tbls chopped fresh parsley
1 cup chopped carrots
1 cup chopped celery
1 cup chopped onion
1 cup coarsely chopped tomato
2 tbls evoo
loaf of crusty bread, thick sliced

1. In a large stockpot over medium-high heat, heat the oil to smoking. Add the carrots, onions and celery and cook stirring, 6-8 minutes. Add the chicken stock, tomatoes, and beans, and bring to a boil. Reduce the heat to low, and add the broccoli. Simmer for 8-10 minutes.
2. Add the tomatoes and the parsley, season with the salt and pepper, and simmer for 10 minutes more.
3. Place some bread slices at the bottoms of soup bowls. Ladle the soup over the bread. Sprinkle with the cheese and serve.

Bruschetta

The word bruschetta comes from the verb bruscare, which translates to char over hot coals. In Italy, it's a standard first course. Bruschetta is often served with nothing more than being rubbed with a clove of garlic and a drizzle of extra virgin olive oil, and served warm. However, there are a lot of variations of bruschetta, both here in America and in Italy. Shrimp, eggplant, fresh mozzarella, olive tapenades, the list is endless. If you don't have hot coals ready, the broiler works just as well. The bread is usually peasant bread, but any crusty bread will do. This recipe is for four.

Fresh Mozzarella and Basil Bruschetta

8 slices crusty bread
1 recipe fresh mozzarella, (page 78), cut into ½ inch slices
16 fresh basil leaves
cvoo
Kosher salt to taste

1. Heat your grill to high (page 9) or light your broiler.
2. Grill the bread on both sides until you get some nice grill marks.
3. Drizzle the bread with the oil. Place a slice of Mozzarella on each slice of bread, and 2 basil leaves. Sprinkle with salt and serve immediately.

Artichoke and Olive Salad

This is a quick tasty salad that can accompany just about anything, especially any bruschetta.

1 (14 oz.) can artichoke hearts, drained
12 black olives
1 small red onion, finely chopped
2 garlic cloves, finely chopped
1 tbls red wine vinegar
¼ cup evoo
Kosher salt and freshly ground black pepper

1. Put the vinegar in a medium bowl and slowly whisk in the oil.
2. Add the rest of the ingredients in the bowl and stir to coat evenly. Cover and refrigerate for at least 2 hours. Serve cold or at room temperature.

Caprese Salad

This is a great summer salad, first course, or like the Italians, the last course.

1 recipe Fresh Mozzarella Cheese (page 78), cut into 1/8 inch slices
4 large tomatoes, cut into ¼ inch slices
½ cup fresh basil leaves
evoo
Kosher salt

1. Arrange the tomato slices on a platter. Place a slice of cheese on the tomato slices.
2. Drizzle the stacks with the oil and sprinkle with the salt.
3. Place 1 or 2 basil leaves, depending on size, on top of the cheese. Serve immediately.

Desserts

Italians, for the most part, aren't big dessert eaters. Despite some of the unique Italian recipes, such as fried wandies and frosted grapes, Italians might just eat a small piece of the local cheese or a piece of fresh fruit after the main course. Quite often a salad is the last course. One of my uncle's favorite desserts was simply a piece of fresh fruit and a couple of ounces of gorgonzola cheese.

This doesn't mean that Italians don't eat dessert at all, but it's not that common. Italians prefer savory flavors at the end of a meal that compliment the main course. Gelato, Italian ice cream, is more often a refreshing afternoon snack rather than dessert.

Crème Fraiche
Perfect Whipped Cream
Buddy's Brandied Bananas
Pears in Red Wine
Cherries in Red Wine
Frosted Grapes
Lemon Italian Ice
Strawberry Italian Ice
Stewed Cinnamon Apples
Zabaglione
Biscotti
Macaroons
Anise Cookies
Gorgonzola Stuffed Pears
Honey Glazed Watermelon

Crème Fraiche

Crème Fraiche is French for fresh cream. It's fresh cream that's allowed to thicken. This makes for more of a mouth feel than whipped cream.

1 cup heavy cream
1 tsp buttermilk or 2 tsp Sour cream.

1. Whisk the ingredients together in a medium bowl. Let stand at room temperature, uncovered for at least 1 day, until thickened.
2. When thick, place in an airtight container refrigerate for up to several weeks.
3. Serve with fruits or ice creams.

Perfect Whipped Cream

The key to perfect whipped cream is to keep the cream ice cold while whipping. This is easily maintained buy using an ice bath.

2 cups heavy cream
1 tsp confectioners' sugar

1. Two hours before whipping, place a large bowl in the refrigerator.
2. When ready to whip, fill a very large bowl halfway with ice and water. Place the refrigerated bowl inside the ice bath. Pour the cream into the bowl and add the sugar. With an electric mixer or balloon whisk, whip the cream until you have stiff peaks. It should double in size.

Whipped cream can be kept in an airtight container for up to 5 days.

Buddy's Brandied Bananas

This is my take on an old classic. It's inexpensive but it tastes expensive. Have your family watch you prepare it. They'll think you've been going to cooking school, especially after you light the pan. If the flame gets too high, put a lid over the flames.

4 ripe bananas
¼ cup (½ stick) unsalted butter
6 tbls dark brown sugar
2 ozs. brandy of you choice
½ tsp cinnamon
½ tsp nutmeg
½ tsp kosher salt

1. Two hours before serving, place four bowls in the refrigerator.
2. On low heat, heat a 12 skillet, preferably cast iron, until smoking. Add the butter and the brown sugar, stirring constantly until you have a thin caramel.
3. Remove the pan from the heat and slowly add the brandy. If it doesn't flame up, use a candle lighter. When the flames go out, add the bananas, cinnamon, nutmeg and salt. Stir or toss the bananas in the sauce and cook for 2 minutes.
4. Remove the bowls from the refrigerator and fill them with the bananas. Top with ice cream, whipped cream or both.

Pears in Red Wine

Traditionally Italians drink wine all day. They also cook with wine, a lot. The only rule is that you don't cook with wine that you wouldn't drink It's a simple delicious dessert or afternoon snack.

½ cup sugar
½ cup water
1 cinnamon stick
½ cup red wine
2 fresh pears, peeled and halved, seeds removed

1. In a medium saucepot over high heat, bring the sugar, water, the cinnamon stick and the wine to a boil. Reduce the heat, add the pears, and simmer for 10-12 minutes.
2. Remove from the heat and serve immediately by itself or with ice cream.

Cherries in Red Wine

1 (29 ounce) can tart red cherries
1 ¼ cup sugar
3 cups red wine of your choice
1 cup whipped cream (page 90)

1. In a medium saucepot over high heat, bring the sugar, water and the wine to a boil. Reduce the heat, add the cherries, and simmer for 10-12 minutes.
2. Serve immediately with the whipped cream.

Frosted Grapes

1 ½ lbs grape clusters
½ cup sugar
½ cup red wine

1. In a small saucepot over medium high heat, dissolve the sugar in the wine and boil for 6-7 minutes.
2. Set up a cooking rack in a large sheet pan. Dip the grape clusters into the syrup and place on the rack. Sprinkle with more sugar and let cool.

Italian Ice

Italian Ice is not lemonade. It is essentially frozen sugar and water with a creamy texture. It's more refreshing than lemonade and just about anything else I can think of. Well beer maybe. This is a great snack anytime, and of course for dessert.

Lemon Ice

2 cups water
1 cup sugar
1 cup fresh lemon juice, 3-4 lemons

1. In a small saucepot over medium high heat, dissolve the sugar in the water and boil for 6-7 minutes. Remove from the heat and cool.
2. When cool, add the lemon juice and stir. Pour the mixture into small plastic containers. Place in the freezer for 4 hours, stirring every half hour. The mixture will have the texture of snow.

Strawberry Ice

1 pint fresh strawberries, washed and hulled
1 cup water
¾ cup sugar
2 tbls fresh lemon juice

1. In a small saucepot over medium high heat, dissolve the sugar in the water and boil for 6-7 minutes. Let cool.
2. Place the strawberries in a food processor and puree.
3. Combine both mixtures and place in small containers. Place in the freezer until firm Will keep covered for up to 1 week.

Note: Any fruit can be used to make Italian Ice, but you will have to adjust for sweetness.

Stewed Cinnamon Apples

I chose apples for this recipe, but pears would work just as well. This is great over ice cream, whipped cream or by itself. It sounds like it would make an excellent pie, also.

4-6 cooking apples
water to cover
3 tbls brown sugar
2 tbls butter
1 tsp cinnamon

1. Peel, core and cut the apples into 1 inch wedges.
2. Place the apples in a saucepot and cover with water. Cook over low heat until tender, 8-10 minutes.
3. Add the sugar, butter and cinnamon and stir to combine. Simmer for 8-10 minutes.

Zabaglione

A simple and elegant Italian custard.

4 egg yolks beaten
½ cup Marsala wine
¼ cup sugar
1 tsp vanilla

1. Place the egg yolks, sugar and the wine in a metal bowl and beat until well blended.
2. Place a pot of water on the stove and bring to a boil. Holding the bowl over the boiling water, (do not let the bowl touch the water) beat the mixture until it is thick, fluffy and light. Blend in the vanilla and serve hot or cold.

Biscotti

Biscotti is quite simple and inexpensive to make. The name comes from *bis,* or twice, and *cotti.* The past participle of the verb "to cook" The second cooking is the step that makes this batter crisp and hard, not soft like a traditional cookie. This is the traditional biscotti recipe. If you would like chocolate biscotti, add cocoa powder, chocolate chips and another ½ cup of sugar.

2 ¼ cups all purpose-flour
1 2/3 cups sugar
3 large eggs + 4 yolks
¾ cup hazelnuts
1 tbls Amaretto
1 tsp baking powder

1. Preheat the oven to 350 degrees.
2. In a large bowl, stir together the flour, sugar and the baking powder. In another bowl, whisk together the eggs, yolks and Amaretto. Add the wet ingredients to the dry and stir just until the dough comes together. Add the hazelnuts and mix to incorporate.
3. Roll the dough into 3 logs. Place on an un-greased baking sheet and bake until lightly browned, about 20 minutes. Remove from the oven and let cool. Lower the oven to 275 degrees. Diagonally cut the logs into 1/3 inch thick pieces. Arrange them cut side down on the same baking pan. Return to the oven and bake for 20 more minutes. Serve when cool.

Macaroons

The secret to a good macaroon is to beat the egg whites long enough, until they form stiff peaks. Obviously, this takes longer, but the result is moister cookies. You also get to use the leftover egg whites from the biscotti.

4 egg whites
2 cups sugar
½ cup finely ground almonds
1 tsp almond extract
½ tsp kosher salt

1. Preheat the oven to 350 degrees.
2. In a large bowl, beat the egg whites with the salt until they are creamy. Using a mixer or a whisk, slowly add the sugar while mixing. Fold in the almonds and the extract, and mix until the dough forms stiff peaks.
3. On a parchment paper lined baking sheet, drop spoonfuls of batter, approximately ¾ inch apart. Bake until lightly browned, 10—12 minutes. Serve warm or cool.

Anise Cookies

3 ½ cups all-purpose flour
4 eggs
1 cup shortening
1 cup sugar
1/3 cup milk
2 tbls anise seed
4 tsps baking powder
1 tsp vanilla

1. Preheat the oven to 375 degrees.
2. In a large bowl, beat the eggs well. Add the sugar, vanilla, milk and the anise seed, and mix well. In another bowl, mix 3 cups of the flour, baking powder and the shortening. Mix in the liquid ingredients. If you don't have a dough consistency batter, add more flour. Roll out the dough and cut into desired shapes.
3. Place on greased cookie sheets and bake 10-12 minutes.

Honey Glazed Watermelon

This is a quick and simple dessert or snack that goes great after a barbecued meal.

4 lbs watermelon chunks
1 cup fresh lime juice
¼ cup honey

1. In a medium saucepan on medium heat, bring the lime juice and the honey to a boil and cook for 2 minutes. Remove from the heat and let cool.
2. When ready to serve, place the watermelon in a large bowl and add the honey syrup. Gently toss the watermelon in the sauce and serve immediately over ice cream or simply by itself.

Gorgonzola Stuffed Pears

Gorgonzola is Italian blue cheese. You can use any blue cheese you like.

4 fresh pears, peeled, halved and cored
3 ozs. Gorgonzola cheese
3 tbls unsalted butter
2 tbls fresh lemon juice
3 tbls finely crushed nuts of your choice

1. Put the lemon juice in a medium bowl. Add the lemon juice and cover the pears with water, and set aside.
2. In another bowl, add the cheese and the butter and cream them together until soft.
3. Fill the center of the pear halves with the cheese mixture. Sprinkle with the nuts. Chill at least one hour before serving.